UNITED STATES AIR FORCE
UNITED STATES AIR FORCE
UNITED STATES AIR FORCE
USAF
USAF
USAF

"WILD BLUE YONDER"

The song "The U.S. Air Force" is the official song of the Air Force. It is also called "Wild Blue Yonder." It was first performed in 1939. Robert MacArthur Crawford wrote the lyrics and music as part of a competition in 1938 by Liberty Magazine. *Air Force wives chose his submission as the winner.*

Off we go into the wild blue yonder,
Climbing high into the sun

★ **AIR FORCE FACTS** The first planes U.S. airmen flew in World War I (1914–1918) were French and British designs. The Lockheed P-80 Shooting Star was the first U.S.-made operational jet fighter. It was made in 1943.

DISCOVER "WILD BLUE YONDER"

A Tribute to the U.S. Air Force

Cherry Lake Press

Published in the United States of America by Cherry Lake Publishing
Ann Arbor, Michigan
www.cherrylakepublishing.com

Reading Adviser: Beth Walker Gambro, MS, Ed., Reading Consultant, Yorkville, IL
Content Adviser: Cory A. Genelin, Lt Col USAF (Ret.)

Photo Credits: U.S. Air National Guard photo by Staff Sgt. Taylor Solberg, cover, title page; U.S. Air Force, 5; © CHARLES PHELPS CUSHING/Alamy, 7; © Science History Images/Alamy; © US Air Force Photo/Alamy, 9; Ethan Johnson/DVIDS/Public Domain, 10; © noraismail/Shutterstock, 11; Dylan Smith/DVIDS/Public Domain, 12; Airman 1st Class Savannah Carpenter/DVIDS/Public Domain, 13; Tech. Sgt. Erik Cardenas/U.S. Air Force, 14; © Felix Lipov/Shutterstock, 15; U.S. Air Force, 16; © Knumina Studios/Shutterstock, 17; 413th Flight Test Group/U.S. Air Force, 18; Master Sgt. Luke Olson/DVIDS/Public Domain, 19; Staff Sgt. Christina Russo/DVIDS/Public Domain, 20; © Satheesh Sankaran/Shutterstock, 22

Cherry Lake Press is an imprint of Cherry Lake Publishing Group

Library of Congress Cataloging-in-Publication Data has been filed and is available at catalog.loc.gov.

Cherry Lake Publishing Group would like to acknowledge the work of the Partnership for 21st Century Learning, a Network of Battelle for Kids. Please visit Battelle for Kids online for more information.

Printed in the United States of America

Note from Publisher: Websites change regularly, and their future contents are outside of our control. Supervise children when conducting any recommended online searches for extended learning opportunities.

TABLE OF CONTENTS

INTRODUCTION

The ground shakes. A sound like thunder roars across a clear blue sky. The fastest and most powerful jets in the world cut through the air. Pilots **maneuver** their jets in perfect formation. The world rushes by in a blur. There is no room for error.

The **Aeronautical** Division of the U.S. Army **Signal Corps** took to the skies in 1909. It was part of the U.S. Army during its early years. The U.S. Air Force became its own branch in 1947.

Today, the U.S. Air Force has around 318,000 **active duty** members. These airmen serve as pilots, communications experts, and lawyers. They are ground controllers, doctors, mechanics, and engineers. More than 200 different careers help make the U.S. Air Force what it is.

Over the years, many have served. Many have died. All should be honored.

Here they come zooming to meet our thunder,
At 'em now, Give 'em the gun!

LOOK

Look at this historical image of airmen. How do they look different from modern airmen you see in this book?

★ **AIR FORCE FACTS** During the Battle of Saint-Mihiel, U.S. air power showed its strength. This was in World War I. General John Pershing and Colonel William "Billy" Mitchell worked with other Allied forces. They brought together the largest air force that had ever gone to battle.

Down we dive, spouting our flame from under,
Off with one helluva roar!

★ **AIR FORCE FACTS** The U.S. Army air forces grew to include 2,253,000 men and women by 1945. Around 1,100 women tested, flew, and transported 12,650 aircraft. They were Women Service Pilots (WASPs).

We live in fame or go down in flame. Hey! Nothing'll stop the U.S. Air Force!

★ **AIR FORCE FACTS** U.S. Air Force pilots fly faster than the speed of sound. Air Force Brigadier General Chuck Yeager was the first human to fly that fast. In 1947, he flew the experimental Bell X-1 aircraft at about 700 miles (1,127 km) per hour.

Brilliant minds fashioned a crate of thunder,
Sent it high into the blue;

ASK QUESTIONS

What technology do you think is key to keeping the Air Force the best in the world? Do some digging to find the answer.

★ **AIR FORCE FACTS** The U.S. Air Force knows that science and technology are key to keeping the U.S. military the best in the world. Its research has advanced the use of lasers, **electromagnetic waves**, and circuits.

Valiant hands blasted the world asunder;
How they lived God only knew!

★ **AIR FORCE FACTS** In a joint mission with NASA in 1967, the U.S. Air Force set a speed record. This record has never been broken. Colonel Pete Knight was the test pilot. He flew a rocket plane Mach 6.7, or 4,520 miles (7,274 km) per hour. The fastest fighter jets today go half that speed.

Boundless souls dreaming of skies to conquer
Gave us wings, ever to soar!

CREATE

Create a poster or brochure about basic training. Include facts about where Air Force **recruits** train, who trains them, and how they train. Share what you learned.

★ **AIR FORCE FACTS** Tens of thousands of new recruits join the Air Force each year. They spend 7.5 weeks in basic military training. They are challenged physically and mentally. They learn tactical and combat skills. They'll need these skills during their service.

With scouts before and bombers galore. Hey!
Nothing'll stop the U.S. Air Force!

★ **AIR FORCE FACTS** The U.S. Air Force operates many types of aircraft. These include fighter planes, helicopters, and bombers. They include attack planes, transport planes, and **tanker** planes. Other aircraft include **unmanned** aircraft and information-gathering planes.

Here's a toast to the host
Of those who love the vastness of the sky,

MAKE A GUESS

What do you think qualifies someone to be an Air Force pilot? Make a guess! Then research to find out if you're right.

"As the most powerful Air Force in the world, we are blessed to have the best and brightest America has to offer."
– Master Sergeant Christopher Greek, 437th Communications Squadron first sergeant

To a friend we send a message
of the brave who serve on high.
We drink to those who gave their all of old

★ **AIR FORCE FACTS** The U.S. Air Force Memorial stands in Arlington, Virginia. It honors the men and women who have served in the Air Force. Three steel spires sweep up from the ground toward the wild blue yonder.

Then down we roar to score
the rainbow's pot of gold.
A toast to the host of those we boast,
the U.S. Air Force!

★ **AIR FORCE FACTS** Chief Master Sergeant Duane Hackney is the most decorated airman in U.S. Air Force history. He served more than 25 years. He earned more than 70 individual awards and decorations.

Off we go into the wild sky yonder,
Keep the wings level and true;

THINK

Think about how the word true is used in the song. What do you think it means? Why do you think being true is important?

★ **AIR FORCE FACTS** The U.S. Air Force Thunderbirds flight demonstration squad flies the F-16 Fighting Falcon jet. These pilots show the skill and precision of the Air Force. They fly for audiences around the world.

If you'd live to be a grey-haired wonder
Keep the nose out of the blue!

★ **AIR FORCE FACTS** Millions of Air Force veterans have served their country. Of all U.S. military veterans, about 17 percent served in the Air Force.

Fly to fight, guarding the nation's border,
We'll be there, followed by more!

★ AIR FORCE FACTS The U.S. Air Force operates bases in 35 states and the District of Columbia. They also operate in countries around the world. Texas and Florida are home to the most Air Force bases. There are eight in Texas and seven in Florida.

"No matter what the conflict of the future looks like, airpower and spacepower will be at its leading edge."

– Secretary of the Air Force Troy Meink, 2025

In echelon we carry on.
Oh, nothing'll stop
the U.S. Air Force!

THE AIRMAN'S CREED

I am an American Airman.
I am a warrior.
I have answered my nation's call.
I am an American Airman.
My mission is to fly, fight, and win.
I am faithful to a proud heritage,
A tradition of honor,
And a legacy of valor.
I am an American Airman,
Guardian of freedom and justice,
My nation's sword and shield,
Its sentry and avenger.
I defend my country with my life.
I am an American Airman:
Wingman, leader, warrior.
I will never leave an Airman behind,
I will never falter,
And I will not fail.

LEARN MORE

BOOKS

Huddleston, Emma. *Jobs in the Air Force*. Minneapolis, MN: Bearport Publishing, 2025.

Jensen, Caroline. *Thunderbirds*. Mankato, MN: Creative Education, 2026.

McKinney, Donna B. *The United States Air Force*. Minneapolis, MN: Bellwether Media, 2025.

WEBSITES

Search these online sources with an adult.

United States Air Force Facts for Kids | Kiddle

Wild Blue Yonder – Anthem of the US Air Force | BulbaBlin | Video

GLOSSARY

active duty (AK-tiv DOO-tee) describing a member of the U.S. Armed Forces who works for the military full-time and can be deployed

aeronautical (er-uh-NAH-tih-kuhl) dealing with the operation of aircraft

echelon (EH-shuh-lahn) flight formation in which the planes are flying together, with one behind and to the side of another

electromagnetic waves (ih-lek-troh-mag-NEH-tik WAYVZ) waves in the electromagnetic field created by a transmitter.

maneuver (muh-NOO-ver) to move

recruits (rih-CROOTS) new members who just joined

Signal Corps (SIG-nuhl KOR) U.S. Army branch that develops and manages systems of information and communication

tanker (TAYN-kuhr) military plane that refuels other planes in flight

unmanned (uhn-MAND) flying vehicle without a pilot on board

valiant (VAL-yuhnt) having or acting with bravery

INDEX